NETFLIX

ABDO
Publishing Company

TECHNOLOGY
PIONEERS

NETFLIX

THE COMPANY AND ITS FOUNDERS

by Marcia Amidon Lusted

Content Consultant
Chris Morris
Freelance Journalist, Technology Specialist
www.chrismorrisjournalist.com

CREDITS

Published by ABDO Publishing Company, PO Box 398166,
Minneapolis, MN 55439. Copyright © 2013 by Abdo Consulting
Group, Inc. International copyrights reserved in all countries.
No part of this book may be reproduced in any form without
written permission from the publisher. The Essential Library™ is a
trademark and logo of ABDO Publishing Company.

Printed in the United States of America,
North Mankato, Minnesota
052012
092012

 THIS BOOK CONTAINS AT LEAST 10% RECYCLED MATERIALS.

Editor: Sue Vander Hook
Series Designer: Emily Love

Library of Congress Cataloging-in-Publication Data
Lusted, Marcia Amidon.
   Netflix : the company and its founders / Marcia Amidon Lusted.
      p. cm. -- (Technology pioneers)
   Includes bibliographical references.
   ISBN 978-1-61783-334-2
   1. Netflix (Firm)--Juvenile literature. 2. Hastings, Reed,
1960---Juvenile literature. 3. Streaming technology
(Telecommunications)--Juvenile literature. I. Title.
   HD9697.V544N485 2013
   384.55'506573--dc23
                                    2012011527

TABLE OF CONTENTS

Chapter 1   Instant Movies   6

Chapter 2   Entertainment Evolution   14

Chapter 3   The Men behind Netflix   24

Chapter 4   Going Live   34

Chapter 5   Connecting with Starz   46

Chapter 6   Deals and More Deals   56

Chapter 7   Original Content   66

Chapter 8   Company Collapse   76

Chapter 9   The Future of Netflix   86

Timeline   96

Essential Facts   100

Glossary   102

Additional Resources   104

Source Notes   106

Index   110

About the Author   112

Reed Hastings, cofounder and CEO of Netflix, was *Fortune* magazine's 2010 Businessperson of the Year.

INSTANT MOVIES

In November 2010, *Fortune* magazine announced its Businessperson of the Year—Reed Hastings, chief executive officer (CEO) of Netflix. Under Hastings's leadership, Netflix had grown rapidly and evolved with changing technology, going from renting DVDs by mail to providing instant streaming of movies, television shows, and television series over the Internet. Now the company was booming. Netflix stock had skyrocketed on the stock exchange. It was "the stock of the year, up more than 200% since January," and the company was expanding into foreign markets.[1]

Fortune magazine called Hastings the "leader of the pack" of a company that should have failed by now.[2] Hastings had toppled the movie rental industry with his ever-changing approach to home entertainment. He had triumphed over all his competitors. The article stated, "Cable companies hate him. Hollywood studios aren't sure whether to embrace him or fend him off."[3] All signs pointed to Netflix getting bigger and bigger. And it had all begun with one person's simple idea.

NEW CUSTOMERS

During the last quarter of 2011, Netflix added 610,000 new US subscribers, bringing the total number of subscribers to 24.4 million.

LITTLE RETURN ENVELOPES

Netflix was founded in 1997, when the Internet was still relatively new. As more and more people began owning personal computers and getting online, Hastings and cofounder Marc Randolph saw an opportunity. They realized many customers who wanted to watch movies at home no longer wanted to drive back and forth to a video store.

Customers were also weary of paying late fees if they did not return their videos on time. With a Netflix account and a small monthly fee, people could rent an unlimited number of movies online and have them mailed directly to their homes. To get started, a person simply had to visit the Netflix Web site, create an account, and make a list of movies he or she wanted to watch.

Netflix mailed the first movie on the list to the customer and included a postage-paid envelope. When finished watching the movie, the customer mailed it back in the little return envelope. Then Netflix mailed out the next movie title in the customer's queue. Netflix subscribers thus had a continuous supply of movies coming to their homes. They could even add movies to their lists that had

A Netflix associate works on DVD rental returns.

not yet been released. Once the movies became available, Netflix shipped them out immediately.

Then, in 2008, Netflix added the online video streaming option. For no additional cost, Netflix customers had the option to stream movies and television shows instantly from the Internet right onto their computers, televisions, and other devices such as smartphones.

"There are three types of customers at Netflix. One group likes the convenience of free home delivery, the movie buffs want access to the widest selection of, say, French New Wave or Bollywood films, and the bargain hunters want to watch 10 or more movies for 18 bucks a month. We need to keep all the audiences happy because the more someone uses Netflix, the more likely they are to stay with us."[4]

—*Reed Hastings*

Netflix seemed to be in a good place. It catered to traditional customers who still watched movies on DVD, and it kept up with those who wanted instant entertainment from the Internet and preferred online streaming.

By the beginning of 2011, it seemed as though Netflix was on top of the world. It was the leading provider of DVD rentals by mail, and its online streaming feature was growing rapidly. Netflix focused on making deals with more and more content providers such as movie studios and television networks to make more movies and television shows available to its customers. It was also building a reputation as a popular distributor of independent films produced by smaller companies or even individuals.

THE CUSTOMERS ARE ANGRY

In the summer of 2011, Netflix made several critical decisions that would threaten the very existence of the company. The decisions were practical for the company, made for financial reasons, but they angered many of Netflix's longtime customers, who felt betrayed by the changes to their service. Customers were upset and began leaving the company in droves, putting the future of Netflix on very shaky ground.

Hastings had gone from being the 2010 *Fortune* magazine Businessperson of the Year to issuing an embarrassing public apology to thousands of angry customers. He would quickly lose a large portion of his own personal fortune, and his company would suffer financially.

TELEVISION IS STILL HERE

Even in this age of digital devices, television is still the primary source of entertainment in American households. In 2011, 44 million television sets were sold in North America. Statistics show shoppers typically purchase a new television set approximately every seven years. However, it is a growing trend for television viewers to watch less broadcast television and more streamed-on-demand television that comes from plugging into a source such as Netflix. Most television viewers today are also multitasking while they watch television. They surf the Internet, go on social networking sites, and text on their cell phones while movies or television shows are playing. Netflix has become one of the top destinations for Americans to access their favorite videos.

Would Netflix survive its growing pains and correct what analysts called the "missteps" made in 2011?[5] And could Netflix maintain its position as the leader in the movie rental and online streaming industry? +

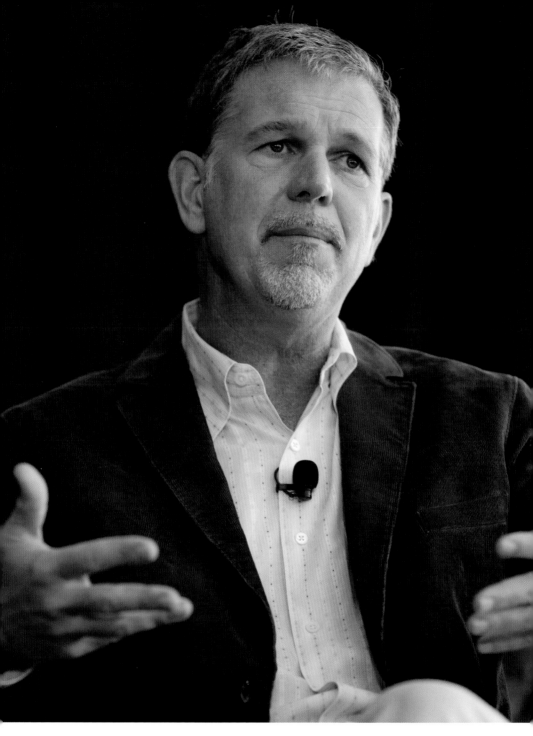

Hastings's decisions in 2011 put Netflix's future in jeopardy.

A crowd gathered outside Warner's Theatre in New York City for the 1926 opening of *Don Juan*, a silent film with synchronized music but no dialogue that led to the breakthrough of the talkie.

ENTERTAINMENT EVOLUTION

The success of Netflix was a direct result of rapid changes in entertainment at the end of the 1990s and beginning of the 2000s. During that time, the world went digital, and the Internet and other new technologies altered the way people watched movies and television. People were beginning to listen to music differently and read magazines, newspapers, and books in a variety of formats. During this evolution, entertainment became easier to access and more immediate, sometimes available nearly instantly.

NOW PLAYING

During the first half of the twentieth century, the main way to watch a movie was to go to a movie theater and see it on the big screen. Movies were first shown in theaters in the early 1900s, and until the 1920s, they were moving pictures without sound. Sometimes a live pianist in the theater provided music to go along with these silent films. The first full-length "talkie," or movie with synchronized sound, was *The Jazz Singer,* released in 1927. Going to the movies became a regular part of the entertainment lives of Americans, and almost every small town had at least

THE JAZZ SINGER

The Jazz Singer, starring Al Jolson, premiered in 1927. It tells the story of a young Jewish man who wanted to become a jazz singer in defiance of his family and religion. As the first full-length "talkie," *The Jazz Singer* spelled the end of the silent movie era of the early twentieth century.

one movie theater. Theaters sometimes ran double features, showing two movies for the price of one.

However, when commercial television programming became available in the United States in 1947, the popularity of television increased and attendance at movie theaters declined. People could enjoy their entertainment in the comfort of their own homes. Television also required just one initial expense: a television set. Eventually, some movie theaters closed or went bankrupt. Several large US movie studios also suffered financially.

Some movies eventually migrated to the small screen, as studios discovered they could earn more revenue by allowing their films to be shown repeatedly on television. Television networks began showing movies such as *Gone with the Wind* (1936) and *The Wizard of Oz* (1939) on a regular cycle.

LET'S GO TO THE MOVIES . . . AT HOME

A new invention debuted in 1956. It would be the start of a major change in how people watched movies. The videotape recorder (VTR), as it was called, recorded and played back television programs and movies. It used a reel-to-reel system in which two-inch (5.08 cm) magnetic tape advanced from

Through the 1940s and 1950s, television quickly
became a popular family pastime.

one exposed reel, or spool, to a second one, as video
and audio from the television were recorded onto
the tape. Once a program was recorded, it could be
played back through the television screen. The first
VTR, sold by Ampex Corporation, cost $50,000.
This was far too expensive for the average consumer,
and only television networks bought them. Then, in
1965, Japanese electronics company Sony introduced
the CV-2000, a reel-to-reel VTR specifically aimed

VHS VS. BETAMAX

In the early days of consumer VCRs, there were two different types of videocassette tapes. The Betamax format, created by Sony in 1975, was considered better in picture quality and video standards. The Video Home System (VHS) had the advantage of a longer recording time. Betamax and VHS competed for customers. In some towns, there was a video rental store that offered Betamax and another that stocked VHS. But ultimately, VHS became the more popular format, and Betamax became obsolete.

at the home consumer market. The CV-2000 allowed individuals to record and play back television programming at home. It was still very expensive, priced at approximately $700, but it was the beginning of a trend.

By the late 1970s and early 1980s, the VTR had evolved into the videocassette recorder (VCR). The VCR's recording tape was encased in a rectangular plastic box that slipped into the machine, which allowed the VCR to be much more compact than a reel-to-reel system. Movie rental stores began opening in nearly every town, allowing customers to rent both new and old movies and watch them at home. Consumers at that time usually did not buy movies because videocassettes were too expensive. But eventually the prices came down, and consumers were able to build their own movie libraries.

The videocassette with exposed videotape was replaced with the digital versatile disc (DVD).

In 1997, a new technology was introduced that would ultimately replace the VCR. The digital versatile disc (DVD) player played movies on a small disc, called a DVD, the same size as a compact disc (CD) typically used for musical recordings. DVDs had an advantage over movies on videotape because they did not have the long strips of magnetic tape that could stretch, break, or tangle inside a VCR. Instead, data was stored on the disc in the form of tiny pits on the surface. A DVD player used a low-powered laser to read the data. The sturdy discs were only 4.7 inches (120 mm) in diameter and could store more data than a videocassette.

However, just like the first VCR, the earliest DVD player was too expensive for the average consumer, and at first there were few movies available for DVD players. But by 2000, DVD players had fallen to an affordable price, and consumers began buying them. That year, more than 13 million American homes had DVD players. Movie stores began adding movies on DVD to their stock of videocassette movies already on the shelves.

I WANT IT NOW

In the mid-1990s, cable television networks began offering subscribers the option to pay extra to watch a movie. This service, called pay-per-view, meant that a cable customer could choose a movie from a list,

LASERDISCS

Besides videocassettes, another early home video format was the LaserDisc, which looked like a larger version of a DVD. It measured nearly 12 inches (30.5 cm) in diameter and was made of aluminum layered in plastic. The first movie to be released on LaserDisc was *Jaws* in 1978. The last movies in this format were produced in 2000. The technology behind LaserDiscs would become the foundation for CDs and DVDs.

agree to the extra charge on his or her monthly bill, and watch the movie on television immediately. There was no waiting and no need to leave home because the movie was delivered through cable. The idea caught on, and many Americans began renting movies through their cable television companies.

In the late 1990s and early 2000s, video streaming on personal computers was available, but few people had fast enough Internet service to support more than brief video clips or short films. Increased Internet speeds eventually allowed users to stream full-length movies, television shows, and radio— first on their personal

STREAMING

Just what is streaming audio and video, and how does it work? Think of it this way: when people talk, their voices travel in the form of sound waves. The human ears and brain receive the information and decode it so it can be understood. A similar process happens with streaming audio or video. First, someone codes the information and makes it available on a computer server. Then, it can be sent through the Internet to a personal computer, which decodes the information and turns it into music or a video that a person can understand. Online streaming got its start in the late 1990s as more and more people began watching videos and listening to music through their computers. At first, streaming was painfully slow, especially if the user had a slow computer or a dial-up Internet connection. The stream of data was often intermittent, or interrupted, creating a choppy image or sound. Today's speedy Internet connections have made streaming faster and of higher quality. People now routinely use Internet streaming to listen to radio broadcasts, watch movies, and catch up on missed episodes of their favorite television shows.

computers and later on smartphones and other handheld devices. Video streaming gave people a new way to expand their entertainment possibilities.

In just a few decades, advances in technology had greatly altered the way Americans enjoyed their entertainment. One person who grew up during this evolution was Hastings. His ideas would change home entertainment even further. +

DVDs began providing home entertainment in the early 2000s.

Hastings graduated from Bowdoin College
in Brunswick, Maine, in 1983.

THE MEN
BEHIND NETFLIX

Wilmot Reed Hastings Jr. was born
October 8, 1960, in Belmont,
Massachusetts, a suburb of Boston.
His father was a lawyer who once worked for

the administration of President Richard Nixon (1969–1974).

As a teenager, Reed attended Buckingham Browne & Nichols, a private high school in Cambridge, Massachusetts. He graduated in 1978 and then took a year off before attending college. During that year, he sold vacuum cleaners door-to-door, cleaning customers' rugs as part of his sales pitch.

BUDDING ENTREPRENEUR

In the fall of 1979, Hastings began his college years at Bowdoin College, a small college in Brunswick, Maine, and majored in mathematics. While he was there, he earned two mathematics department prizes: the Smyth Prize in 1981 and the Hammond Prize in 1983. He also organized hiking and canoeing trips as the head of Bowdoin's Outing Club.

Hastings graduated from Bowdoin in 1983. He left early on his graduation day in order to attend training for the Peace Corps. His first assignment was at a high school with 800 students in northwest Swaziland, a country in southern Africa. Hastings credits his experiences in Swaziland for helping him later become a successful business entrepreneur. He

THE PEACE CORPS

The Peace Corps is a volunteer organization run by the US government. It was founded in 1961 by President John F. Kennedy with the mission of providing technical assistance to other countries in need, helping people outside the United States to understand US culture, and helping Americans understand the cultures of other countries. Since it was founded, more than 200,000 Americans have served in the Peace Corps in 139 countries.

said, "Once you have hitchhiked across Africa with ten bucks in your pocket, starting a business doesn't seem too intimidating."[1]

Hastings stayed in the Peace Corps until 1985, when he decided to go back to school. He attended Stanford University in California and earned a master's degree in computer science in 1988. After graduating, he landed his first job in the business world with Schlumberger, where he worked as a member of the company's technical staff in Palo Alto, California. His next job was debugging software for a start-up company called Coherent Thought. In 1991, at the age of 31, he started his own business, Pure Software.

Pure Software initially offered just one product, a debugging tool called Purify. Then the company added two more products: Quantify and Purelink. They were so popular that Pure Software doubled the amount of money it was making every year for four years.

Hastings enjoyed the excitement of the early days of Pure Software, but as the company grew, he felt it became boring and bureaucratic, just like any other established company. According to an article in *Bloomberg Businessweek*, Hastings felt the company "went from being a heat-filled, everybody-wants-to-be-here place to a dronish, when-does-the-day-end sausage factory."[2]

His boredom with Pure Software would lead Hastings to think carefully about what his next company would be like. Pure Software had never had time to develop its own culture because it grew too quickly, and Hastings realized he had helped build a company he really did not want any part of. In 1996, Pure Software merged with Atria Software and became Pure Atria Software. In August 1997, Hastings sold the company for $750 million, which made him a very wealthy man. He would use that money to fund his next venture.

One employee who worked for Hastings at Pure Atria was Vice President of Corporate Marketing Marc Randolph. Randolph would soon become a key player in Hastings's next move.

A CORPORATE CLIMB

Born on April 29, 1958, Randolph was a seasoned marketing professional when he went to work for Hastings. Leadership and communications figured prominently in Randolph's life from an early age. A key formative experience came when Randolph was 14. His parents sent him to a 30-day outdoor leadership camp in Wyoming run by the National Outdoor Leadership School. As he explained, "It was there in Wyoming that I learned almost everything I know about being an entrepreneur."[3]

Randolph attended Hamilton College in Clinton, New York. Perhaps his early love of mountains and the outdoors

OUTDOOR LEADERSHIP

Randolph was inspired by the time he spent at the National Outdoor Leadership School (NOLS) as a teen. He later said, "NOLS taught me to be a leader. Not by telling me how to do it, but by letting me practice being one."[4] As each camper took turns leading the day's hike, Randolph learned that the leader's choices determined whether they had an exhilarating day or an exhausting one. When he took his turns, he realized being the leader was not about having all the answers. Instead, the most important leadership skills he learned were listening to others, sifting through the information, making a decision, and expressing that decision. Performing these actions effectively would make others into more willing followers.

Randolph has remained connected to NOLS since his first camp experience. He took multiple courses, progressing to become a class instructor. As of 2012, Randolph was a member of the NOLS board of trustees.

influenced his decision to major in geology. He later said two of the most important classes he ever took were during his freshman year at Hamilton: public speaking and basic composition. A passion for communicating would serve him well in his later career. He graduated from Hamilton in 1981.

Randolph's marketing career took off within years of graduation. By 1986, he was working in Silicon Valley as vice president of direct marketing for Borland International, a software company. He was a fish out of water in some ways, a marketer and communicator surrounded by engineers. He realized, however, that for a tech company to be successful, the engineers needed someone to communicate their vision to consumers and nontechnical people. Randolph would spend the next decade of his career with several companies serving as that communicator, ending up with Hastings at Pure Atria in 1996.

A NEW VENTURE

After he sold Pure Atria, Hastings decided to once again further his own education. He returned to Stanford University to pursue a master's degree in education.

The rental of a movie in 1997 was the spark
that ignited the idea of Netflix.

As Hastings was working on his degree, business
was still on his mind. He was a rich man without
a company to keep him occupied, and soon he was
thinking about what his next start-up venture might
be. The idea that would become Netflix started in
late 1997 when Hastings rented the movie *Apollo 13*
from a video rental store and then misplaced it. The
date it was due came and went, and Hastings still
could not find it.

When the video was six weeks late, he finally
located it but had to pay a late fee of $40. Hastings
called the ordeal a little embarrassing:

I didn't want to tell my wife. Because you know I knew what she would say. Just like, you know, an eye roll. An eye roll that could kill! And I thought, "Oh, great! Now I'm thinking about lying to my wife about a late fee and the sanctity of my marriage for this thing!" I mean it was just crazy. And I was on the way to the gym and I realized—"Whoa! Video stores could operate like a gym, with a flat membership fee." And it was like "I wonder why no one's done that before!"[5]

Hastings's idea was simple: use the Internet to host a video rental service with no due dates and no late fees. A person could rent a movie through the Web site, and the company would deliver the movie right to the customer's door by US mail. And thus the idea of Netflix was born.

At the time, DVD technology with its small, slim disc design was just becoming available, and Hastings realized he could take advantage of the new format. Flat, slim DVDs would be much cheaper and easier to mail than bulky videocassettes. But first, Hastings had to make sure the DVDs would not get damaged in the mail. "I . . . bought a bunch and mailed them to myself and then I waited," he said. "And I opened them up. And they were fine.

And I thought, . . . 'This is gonna work! This is gonna work!'"[6]

To help develop the company that would become Netflix, Hastings enlisted Randolph. There were many details to iron out, and they were not sure the idea would work. Most people were still watching movies on videocassettes and used a dial-up phone connection to access the Internet. Video rental stores were just beginning to carry DVDs, and DVD players still cost as much as $700 apiece, a price too high for most consumers.

But by the time Netflix was ready to market its service, DVD players were more affordable, and video rental stores were starting to stock their shelves with movies on DVD. Internet speeds were becoming faster, which was making it easier for people to navigate online. Potential customers of the new venture would be able to quickly choose a movie they wanted to see from the Netflix Web site. Would the idea catch on? Would it work? +

"Netflix is a powerful idea—one that combines old-timey mail, newfangled Internet, freedom of choice, and our God-given right to be lazy."[7]

—*Stacey Grenrock Woods,* Esquire *magazine*

Randolph, *rear*, brought marketing savvy to Netflix.

DVDs were prepared for shipping at Netflix's first
distribution center in San Jose, California.

GOING LIVE

P roduced by Randolph, the Netflix Web site
went live on April 14, 1998. Randolph served
as the first CEO and Hastings was chairman of
the board of directors. However, by 1999, Hastings
became CEO and Randolph moved into the role

of executive producer. Randolph would retire from the company entirely in 2004.

The company opened a distribution facility in San Jose, California, in 1998. At first, Netflix worked like a video store, except everything was handled by mail. Hastings explained, "Early on, the first concept we launched was rental by mail, but it . . . worked more like Blockbuster. Some people liked it, but it wasn't very popular."[1] Customers ordered one movie at a time on the Netflix Web site and paid one price per movie. Movies cost four dollars for each rental and two dollars for shipping. Additional titles on the same order cost three dollars each and one dollar for shipping.

Netflix's main challenge was how to mail DVDs back and forth economically. Even one extra ounce made the cost of postage increase. DVDs were light and easy to mail but had to be packaged securely so they would not break in transit. Customers also needed an easy way to return DVDs once they finished watching their movies.

WHAT'S IN A NAME?

Randolph considered a variety of names for the company before everyone agreed on Netflix. Some discarded names included Directpix, Webflix, and E-Flix.

MOVIES IN THE MAIL

Netflix's solution to the problem was to develop an envelope that was strong enough to protect DVDs and light enough to require minimal postage. The envelope also had to be durable enough to lie around someone's house until the customer watched the movie and was ready to slip it back in the envelope to return it. The first mailer was made out of sturdy white cardboard.

Mailing movies back and forth was not very profitable for Netflix. The box with the DVD inside weighed more than one ounce, so it required extra postage. Hastings remarked, "We were a typical Internet

THROTTLING

As Netflix was getting started, some of its methods made customers unhappy. One was called "throttling," a technique that gave first priority to customers who rented less frequently in an attempt to get them to rent more often. The most in-demand movies were offered first to these less active customers, while more frequent Netflix users had to wait for the movies to become available. Throttling got Netflix in trouble when a group of Netflix customers sued the company in a class-action lawsuit, *Frank Chavez v. Netflix, Inc.* The case was settled in 2005 in favor of the customers. As part of the settlement, Netflix gave them a month of free service and added the following language to its terms of service: "In determining priority for shipping and inventory allocation, we may utilize many different factors, including the number and type of DVDs you rent through our service, the membership plan you select, as well as other uses of our service by you."[2] The language would protect them from further lawsuits over this issue.

company back then … an ugly financial story, with not much hope of breaking even."[3] Hastings believed Netflix needed a new way to deliver movies if the company was going to survive. He admitted that "this whole thing could go down" if he could not come up with a better way for the company to make money.[4] Then he added, "Let's try the more radical subscription idea."[5]

Hastings proposed they charge customers a set fee per month to rent as many movies as the customers wanted. It was the same idea Hastings had first considered when he thought about gym memberships and how one fee per month gave him unlimited time in the gym. He was willing to bank on this idea, believing it would change Netflix enough to keep it alive. "We knew it wouldn't be terrible," he said, "but we didn't know if it would be great."[6]

Netflix launched its subscription service on September 23, 1999, with a month's free trial. For a flat fee,

TAKING IT BACK

When Netflix was first starting out, stock analyst Michael Pachter called it "a worthless piece of [trash]" and valued the stock at only $3, even though it was selling for $11 at the time. A black poster with Pachter's picture and his comment on it now hangs on a wall outside a kitchen at Netflix headquarters. More recently, Pachter has said he regrets his comment and admits that Hastings is "clearly a visionary."[7]

Netflix came up with an envelope that was lightweight and protected the DVDs.

customers could rent an unlimited number of movies each month. Netflix mailed up to three DVDs at a time. Whenever a customer returned a DVD, Netflix sent out the next movie in the queue. Within one month, 80 percent of Netflix's customers had switched from the free trial to a paid subscription.

WHAT TO WATCH

When Netflix first began, many people were skeptical. After all, Netflix only rented DVDs, and most people were still watching movies on videocassette. And why would anyone want to wait to get a movie rental by mail, when there seemed to be a movie rental store—and often several—in every neighborhood and town in America? But Netflix did succeed, especially once it switched to a subscription model rather than renting one movie at a time.

One of the reasons Netflix was successful was because, unlike most neighborhood movie rental stores, it did not charge a late fee.

STEALING NETFLIX ENVELOPES

One drawback to Netflix's recognizable envelopes is that they are vulnerable to theft. People, including postal employees, often steal the envelopes along with the DVDs inside. One magazine reported that a postal worker in Colorado stole 503 DVDs before he was caught and arrested.

Customers could keep movies as long as they wanted with no penalty. Netflix also offered more than just new movies to rent. The company actively stocked the distribution facility with older and hard-to-find movies. Most movie rental stores had a stock of 70 percent new movies, but for Netflix, 70 percent of its stock was old movies. For people interested in something besides the recent releases, Netflix was their source. Netflix was the easiest way to find titles that movie rental stores did not stock.

THE WEB SITE

Part of Netflix's success was the way it kept fine-tuning its Web site to make it easier for consumers to navigate. Customers could search for a movie by title, genre, actor, or specific search terms. The site displayed available movies as thumbnail pictures. When a user hovered over a thumbnail with the mouse pointer, a more detailed description of the movie popped up.

Users could build long queues of movies they wanted to see. As soon as one movie was returned, the next one in the queue was automatically mailed out. Netflix then established 58 distribution centers in several parts of the country so mailing times could be shortened and customers would receive their next movie in just a day or two. Of course, extremely rare or exceptionally popular newly released movies sometimes required a longer wait, since there were fewer copies available. But overall, Netflix met its customers' needs, and the number of subscribers grew.

WORKING FOR NETFLIX

Working for Netflix was a different and often pleasant experience. Because of Hastings's past experience with Pure Atria and the lack of unity among its employees, he worked to create a unique atmosphere for the Netflix employees. He still expected high performance from all his management staff—a push for success that had earned him the nickname the Animal—but he wanted to avoid burnout and high turnover. He paid his employees well and gave them unlimited vacation time and generous benefits packages. In return, he required hard work and results. Hastings described this approach as "performance, freedom, and responsibility."[8]

COMPANY CULTURE

Part of Netflix's success comes from the company's internal corporate culture, which some say makes it an appealing place to work. According to Siddharth Anand, an engineer at Netflix, every new employee meets with Hastings himself within a few weeks of being hired to hear him explain what the company's values are. Anand says, "[Netflix] has been the best place I have ever worked. It has this very unique culture that no other company has."[9]

In 2002, the success of Netflix made it a company in which the public wanted to invest. That year, Netflix offered its shares for sale on the stock exchange. Its customer base grew and so did the company's revenue. In 2003, Netflix added its 1 millionth subscriber. But Hastings knew that in order to keep Netflix strong, he would need to stay one step ahead in technology. Netflix had gambled

THE CINEMATCH PROCESS

CineMatch works through a four-step computerized process. First, the computer searches the CineMatch database for people who have rated the same movie. Next, it determines which of those same people have also rated a second movie. Then the computer calculates the statistical likelihood that people who liked the first movie will also like the second movie. Finally, CineMatch establishes a pattern among subscribers' ratings of many films.

on DVD technology and the Internet when it started. What would the company do next?

LET ME RECOMMEND

Netflix added some features to its service that became very popular. On the Web site, subscribers could rate movies with a system of stars. That way, they could let their friends know what they had rented and also see what their friends were watching. The site could also recommend movies a customer might like based on what he or she had rented in the past. To do this required an algorithm Netflix dubbed CineMatch.

CineMatch looked at three things in order to make recommendations. First, it looked at available movies, which were arranged into groups by type. Then it looked at what customers had rented, what was in their queue, and how they had rated movies from one to five stars. Finally, the algorithm looked at the combined ratings of certain movies. Netflix claimed that CineMatch was able to predict which movies a subscriber would like and guess within half a star what rating the user would give each one. The recommendation system steered users to lesser-known movies and decreased the demand for new releases.

The recommendation system was working well, but Netflix still wanted to improve it. In 2006, the company launched a contest offering $1 million to any individual or team that could create a new algorithm that would perform better than CineMatch. Netflix provided contest entrants with the data they needed to test the movies customers watched. The data, which was anonymous, included 100 million customer movie ratings.

SECOND NETFLIX PRIZE

Netflix's first Netflix Prize contest was so successful that the company decided to hold a second round with a more difficult objective. Instead of creating an algorithm based only on customers' ratings of movies, programmers were challenged to include demographics and rental history. This means that the algorithm would include the user's age, gender, zip code, and last 20 rentals. But because the challenge would involve Netflix releasing customers' personal information, the Federal Trade Commission (FTC) stopped the competition and sued Netflix. The contest was canceled.

The $1 million prize was attractive, and groups of computer enthusiasts and experts formed to work on the challenge. Three years later, two teams met Netflix's goal and came up with algorithms that improved on what CineMatch could do by 10 percent. But one team submitted its algorithm ten minutes before the other team, thus winning the million-dollar prize. The team, which called itself BellKor's Pragmatic Chaos, had seven members; two of them were researchers for telephone company AT&T.

The new algorithm improved Netflix's recommendation system. It helped subscribers expand their movie-viewing tastes and brought new attention to more obscure independent films and movies that had been overlooked at the box office, allowing these films to compete with the large Hollywood blockbusters. Netflix was now a major avenue for distributing movies, rivaling theaters and traditional movie rental stores. +

Hastings presents a medal to one of the winners of the $1 million prize.

The Netflix headquarters is in Los Gatos, California.

CONNECTING
WITH STARZ

B y 2006, Netflix was firmly established as one of the easiest ways to rent movies. The process of sending the envelopes back and forth was simple, almost effortless. Little had changed in the process other than the look of the envelope. Netflix redesigned the envelope 12 times before it came up with the little red envelope that became a symbol of the company. Details of the envelope's construction and materials were kept secret so no other company could copy it. The easily recognizable envelope helped with advertising, and most important, it was a cost-effective, easy way to carry out the heart of the business—sending DVDs back and forth through the mail.

Subscribers clearly liked Netflix, and its customer base continued growing as DVD technology became more affordable and widespread. But Hastings was aware that entertainment technology was changing rapidly, and movies were no exception. Before long, the little red envelope was not the only way Netflix customers would be able to receive their favorite movies. They would be able to watch almost anything they wanted instantly through online streaming.

STREAMING

By 2007, faster Internet connections were more widespread, making it possible for people to stream video content onto their personal computers. Netflix began offering a service called Watch

DOWNLOADING OR STREAMING?

What is the difference between downloading and streaming? When a person downloads a file, a copy of the file is retrieved from another location and stored on the individual's computer. Streaming is different because the file is not copied and saved. A stream of data travels from a server to a person's computer so he or she can view it, but it does not stay on the computer's hard drive. It comes, and then it goes.

Instantly that allowed a customer to choose a movie on the Web site and stream it to a computer or television. Watching a movie through streaming was almost instantaneous. When the service debuted in January 2008, it was free to subscribers who had a computer and an Internet connection that was fast enough to support online streaming.

At first, Netflix used a software program called Microsoft Silverlight as a platform for its streaming. This limited the service to computers that could download and run the software. Netflix did not make every movie in its inventory available for streaming, and many titles continued to be available only on DVD. Most consumers were happy with the new technology. They liked having two options: to rent movies by mail or stream them from the Internet.

The new content streaming deal benefited Netflix and Starz.

THE STARZ DEAL

Online streaming became very popular with Netflix customers. But the company still looked for other ways to add value to its services and entice more customers to join. Netflix announced in September 2008 that it made separate deals with the CBS network and the Walt Disney Co. to stream some of the shows aired on CBS, ABC, and the Disney Channel. In October, Netflix announced a partnership with the premium cable television channel Starz. The movie channel, which had debuted in 1994, broadcast new movies and produced some of its own programming. Starz already had its own online subscription movie service called Starz Play. In its deal with Netflix, Starz allowed Netflix customers to stream the Starz Play content without paying any additional fee beyond their Netflix subscription rate.

The addition of Starz Play to Netflix's offerings added 2,500 movies to the Netflix online streaming library. Netflix customers could now choose from more than 12,000 movies and television shows as well as being able to stream the Starz television channel for free. Starz president Bill Myers commented, "Netflix has grown to be an innovative leader in

CLOUD STORAGE

Once Netflix began offering online streaming to its customers, traffic on the Netflix server increased dramatically, and the company needed to change the way it managed, stored, and transferred data. In 2008, Netflix was operating its Web site from just one place. If that location lost power or went offline, it would interrupt service for millions of customers. The answer was for Netflix to adopt a cloud-based storage system. Cloud storage allows network servers to store data in other locations on servers owned by other companies. If a crash occurs in one location, the others can most likely handle the demand, and the chances of losing important data are minimized. Today, when a Netflix customer clicks on "play" for an instant movie, the movie most likely comes from AWS, Amazon.com's cloud service. Amazon.com is also one of Netflix's competitors in providing streaming video.

the home video space. . . . This agreement is a strong vehicle to promote the Starz brand."[1]

While Netflix did not disclose how much it paid Starz to use its content, some estimates ran around $30 million. The deal was very profitable for Netflix. With all the new content, Netflix was able to entice more customers to use its online streaming service, Watch Instantly. Ultimately, the company also hoped to save money by expanding the streaming aspect of its business, as it was less costly to provide instant streaming than to buy and ship DVDs to customers.

GROWING PAINS

As Netflix grew and expanded its services, it worked to keep its customer base happy. One of the features subscribers liked was online user profiles. This feature was popular with families, since it made it possible for one account to have multiple user profiles. For example, a family of four could maintain four separate profiles, each with its own queue according to the family member's taste in movies.

Parents could also restrict what movies their children were allowed to rent. Hastings said at the time,

Families make up a large part of our subscriber base and for them ease, convenience and flexibility are paramount. With Profiles, we have made renting movies even easier for families, ensuring that each member has the movie that is right for them at all times.[2]

"We want to change the world. . . . Reaching consensus is not the most important thing. It's all about taking a stand, making it work, showing it working. If it doesn't work you learn from your mistakes."[3]

—*Siddharth Anand, Netflix engineer*

In 2008, Netflix announced it would eliminate the Profiles feature and remove the additional profiles from existing accounts. The company claimed the feature was complicated and cumbersome to use, since each person with a profile had to log in separately to the account. Netflix said it was making the change to keep the service as simple and easy to use as possible.

Customer feedback was immediate and negative. Users were angry they would lose their profile information. They were also upset that the change would make it harder for the members of a family to share one account. Family members had become accustomed to their own profiles with their favorite movies. Having only one profile for the entire family would force some families to have to pay for multiple accounts. Subscribers saw this change only as a way for Netflix to make more money. Netflix customers were very unhappy and created online petitions that urged users to either put their Netflix accounts on hold or cancel them.

Less than two weeks after Netflix announced the elimination of the Profiles feature, the company changed its mind due to overwhelming customer dissatisfaction. Netflix explained its decision on the company's blog: "We were persuaded by the well-reasoned, sincere responses of loyal members who very much value this feature."[4] The blog went on to say,

Because of an ongoing desire to make our website easier to use, we believed taking a feature away that is only used by a very small minority would help us improve the site for everyone. Listening to our members, we realized that users of this feature

often describe it as an essential part of their Netflix experience.[5]

Netflix had heard its customers' complaints and had responded. Now, the company had to fix its mistake. The feature was restored, but this would not be the last time Netflix would have to respond to negative consumer feedback. It had only begun to see what customer complaints would do to the company. +

NETFLIX   Home   **Just for Kids** ▾   Genres ▾   New Arrivals

Avatar   Phineas & Ferb   Dora   Fairly OddParents

Adventures

Wild Kingdom

  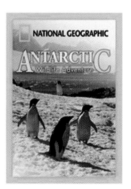 

The Netflix "Just for Kids" Web page gave parents the option of controlling the movies their children ordered.

Microsoft executive Steve Ballmer discusses his company's
partnership with Netflix.

DEALS AND
MORE DEALS

Always looking to create a bigger and better
selection for its customers, Netflix began
making deals with other companies to boost
its online streaming offerings. In 2008, Netflix
partnered with Microsoft to provide movie services

to Microsoft Xbox 360 users who played games online through Xbox Live. Microsoft's deal with Netflix allowed Xbox Live users to access a Netflix queue, browse the library, and stream a movie through the Xbox 360 console.

MORE DEALS

In 2010, Netflix made a five-year deal with EPIX, a network launched in 2009 by movie companies Paramount, MGM, and Lionsgate. The deal allowed Netflix customers to stream all the new movies on the EPIX network 90 days after the movies first aired. It was reported that it cost Netflix $1 billion to form the coalition. The deal provided Netflix customers with one more way to access new movies through online streaming.

Overall, deals made with various networks and movie companies would cost Netflix $180 million in 2010 alone.

FEARFUL MOVIE INDUSTRY

The success of Netflix has created fears in the movie industry that sales of DVDs will fall due to online streaming provided by Netflix. There are also fears that fewer consumers will subscribe to cable television. The movie and television industries see Netflix as a problem and closely watch what the company is doing.

But the company hoped those changes would eventually save money by reducing the cost of producing and shipping DVDs by mail. Over the next few years, Netflix made similar deals with Sony Pictures, Walt Disney Motion Pictures Group, and Overture Films. It also held the rights to stream older movies from the backlists of companies such as Warner Brothers, Paramount, MGM, Universal, and 20th Century Fox.

As Netflix was adding thousands of movies and new sources of online streaming, it also redesigned its Web site and made changes to some of its standard features. Again, one of the changes, a modification to the Friends feature, caused dissatisfaction and controversy among Netflix users.

THE IMITATORS

The success of Netflix has inspired many imitators to use the same business model of a flat subscription fee and revolving rentals. GameFly has a similar service that rents games for gaming consoles such as Xbox, Wii, and PlayStation. In addition to letting users rent games, GameFly also gives users the option of purchasing those games for $15 to $45. Other rental businesses have also started using Netflix's model and example. Booksfree, which rents paperback books and audiobooks through the mail for a monthly flat fee, sends its customers a new book as soon as the previous one is returned. These imitators of Netflix have experienced great success largely because they have followed the Netflix model. Netflix does have a patent for its model, titled "Method and Apparatus of Renting Items." As of 2012, Netflix had not enforced its patent against other types of imitator rental services.

GOOD-BYE, FRIENDS

For years, Netflix users had been able to easily see how their friends in the Netflix network rated a movie. They could also access their friends' Top Ten lists of favorite movies. The Friends feature originally debuted as a way for Netflix to take advantage of the growing popularity of social networking. Friends could connect on Netflix and leave each other notes or film recommendations in their Netflix accounts.

When Netflix redesigned its Web site, users could no longer see their friends' ratings on the page of a particular movie. Instead, they had to access a link at the bottom of the movie page. All this was a preface to Netflix completely phasing out the Friends feature.

Once again, users were quick to express anger at the change. One user wrote,

My friends could easily leave me notes about movies they knew I'd like, and I would do the same. Before deciding to queue a movie, I could see if my friends had seen it and this would help influence my decision.[1]

The user went on to criticize Netflix and threaten to leave the service:

HULU

One of Netflix's biggest competitors in online video streaming—Hulu—already existed when Netflix entered the market in 2008. Hulu had been operating for a year, providing television shows with both free and subscription-only content. For a while, the two companies had different objectives, with Netflix focusing mostly on movies and Hulu on television. But over time, their businesses started to overlap, and both companies offered online streaming of television and movies. Both businesses face competition from network television, which has begun to stream some of its most popular shows online.

I have always been a HUGE proponent of Netflix and have brought a few customers onto the service. One of the reasons I NEVER considered switching to a different service (until now!) was because of all my Netflix friends. Now there's nothing holding me back from going somewhere else.[2]

Netflix had been influenced in the past by customer backlash. This time, however, Netflix would not change its plan to remove Friends. The company cited the fact that only 2 percent of its subscribers used the Friends feature, and it was costing too much of the company's money to maintain it for such a small group. Users retaliated by posting criticism on the movie reviews section of the Web site.

COMPETITION

Netflix continued to be popular despite user criticism. But meanwhile, new competitors had emerged in the market. As early as 2002, retailer Walmart launched an online movie rental service. By 2005, it gave up on the venture and arranged a deal with Netflix instead to promote each other's businesses.

One of Netflix's biggest competitors throughout the years was the Blockbuster movie rental chain. Although Blockbuster began as a movie rental store, it launched its own at-home monthly movie subscription service in 2004, starting a price war with Netflix. That year, Netflix had just raised its monthly subscription price to $21.99 a month. Blockbuster debuted its movie subscription service at $19.99 a month and then reduced it to $17.49. Netflix responded by lowering its price to

THE VALUE OF STOCKS

In 2004, Netflix slashed its prices for the DVD rental plan and spent large amounts of money in order to compete with Blockbuster. While customers were happy, stock prices fell 72 percent. However, people who bought Netflix shares at that rock-bottom price made a great deal of money when the stock increased in value again.

A Blockbuster store closed in New York City in August 2010 after facing competition from video mail order companies such as Netflix.

$17.99, and Blockbuster countered with $14.99 a month. Netflix matched the price with a new two-disc plan at $14.99. But Blockbuster never caught up to Netflix. It was said that the incredible success of Netflix drove Blockbuster into bankruptcy in March 2010. Many Blockbuster stores, as well as other large movie rental chains such as Movie Gallery, closed their doors.

Walmart reentered the competition in 2010 by purchasing the Vudu movie streaming service, a Netflix competitor. Some traditional movie rental stores survived by changing their policies to be more like Netflix, offering their customers a flat subscription rate that would allow them to take out a certain number of movies at a time with no late fees. Another company, Redbox, found a way to rival the convenience of Netflix by placing red movie rental kiosks all over the country on the inside and outside of grocery stores, convenience stores, and similar businesses. Customers select a movie on a screen, swipe a credit card in a slot in the red box, and wait for a DVD to come out in a thin, plastic box. It was rumored that Redbox was going to start its own online movie rental system

REDBOX

Redbox has become Netflix's competitor, particularly for people who do not want to commit to a subscription plan. A Netflix executive, Mitch Lowe, even left the company to become president of Redbox in 2003. Redbox believes it can meet customers' entertainment needs by distributing DVDs. But as online streaming becomes more popular, the company is considering the possibility of offering that service to its customers. Redbox has more than 29,000 kiosks across the United States. Lowe resigned from Redbox in July 2011 to pursue other interests.

with help from its parent company Verizon, but it had not happened as of 2012.

Despite competition, Netflix seemed to be on top of the movie rental business, catering to both traditional DVD customers and those who wanted to receive movies through online streaming. But as before, Hastings and his team were looking for new avenues for Netflix. They wanted to keep the company current and interesting. +

Movie rentals remained Netflix's major business, but Hastings
continued to seek the next great idea.

Visionary leader Hastings has always tried out new ideas
and weathered the occasional failures.

ORIGINAL
CONTENT

I n November 2010, when Hastings became
Fortune magazine's Businessperson of the Year,
the magazine featured an article about him and
Netflix. The article marveled about the unlikely
success of Netflix:

Reed Hastings isn't supposed to be here—not on a list of the year's top businesspeople, and certainly not on the cover of Fortune. *His DVD-by-mail company, Netflix, was supposed to have flamed out by now, a one-trick pony that was destined to be crushed by Blockbuster or Wal-Mart or Apple or you name it. He and his little red envelopes were supposed to be long gone, with Hastings toiling at some new startup, or perhaps enjoying an early retirement in Santa Cruz, Calif., the laid-back seaside city he calls home.[1]*

Netflix was, indeed, an unlikely business to experience such incredible success. Netflix, which many thought would not last more than a few years, was making $2.1 billion a year. Company stock was up more than 200 percent, and the number of subscribers was increasing rapidly. While new competitors were springing up to compete with Netflix, Hastings was certain his company would continue to stay on top. He told *Fortune,*

> *We are in a new race, and we are a player with some very large and substantial [companies] . . . Just to be in that league is an amazing place from where we were.[2]*

PARTNERING WITH FILM COMPANIES

Netflix made some worthwhile new deals in 2011. It entered into an agreement with DreamWorks Entertainment for exclusive rights to broadcast its films and television specials beginning in 2013. DreamWorks, established in 1994, is a very successful film studio owned largely by film director, producer, and screenwriter Steven Spielberg. The company has profited mainly from successful dramas such as *Saving Private Ryan* and animated movies such as *Shrek*.

Netflix also made a deal with Open Road Films, a new movie distribution company based in Hollywood, California, and created by movie theater operators AMC and Regal. Open Road hoped to acquire up to ten movies per year for distribution.

The company gave Netflix exclusive rights to stream its films during what is called the "pay TV window." This is the period of time that starts six to eight months after a movie is released in theaters and lasts about a year. The time frame is when movies are traditionally shown on pay television channels such as HBO and Showtime. Open Road's decision to go with Netflix marked a change in how movies are usually licensed. Relativity Media and Film District, two other movie studios, entered into similar deals with Netflix.

THE NEXT THING

But as always, Hastings was not content to simply let Netflix stay where it was. He knew he always needed to be thinking about the next new thing for his company. He planned to continue licensing more and more existing movies and television shows. Hastings also wanted to expand the offerings of Netflix's Watch Instantly program by acquiring original content.

In March 2011, Netflix announced it was entering the field of producing original content. It outbid several cable television networks, including

HBO, for the rights to the new dramatic series *House of Cards*, starring actor Kevin Spacey. Netflix paid an estimated $100 million for 26 episodes, or two seasons of the show. Netflix was not actually paying to create the show but rather paying for the rights to be the first to show it on the air. This was a new approach, since Netflix had previously only shown content that had already been seen in theaters, on television, and sometimes on DVD. The company hoped the original content would bring a new audience of people to Netflix—the ones who wanted to be the first to see a television series. *TechCrunch*, a Web site with news of the latest in technology, wrote, "With *House of Cards*, the game changes. For the first time, they're going to get people signing up to Netflix to get first access to content."[3] The article went on to say:

> And if it's as good as the talent behind it suggests, they might get a lot of people signing up for that very reason. And if that's the case, they'll be doing a lot more of these deals. And that would effectively make them a premium cable television channel— like HBO or Showtime. But they'll be one with thousands more pieces of content for a lower

BUNDLING

Netflix has entered many partnerships with television, video game console, and handheld device manufacturers to bundle Netflix with their new equipment. Bundling is selling more than one product as a single item. For example, the Netflix partnership with Philips resulted in Philips televisions coming with Netflix already enabled so users can connect directly to the Netflix Web site and access their accounts.

monthly price. And they'll be one not burdened by any artificial show times.[4]

Following its announcement of the acquisition of *House of Cards*, Netflix took it a step further. The company agreed to produce new episodes of the Emmy-winning sitcom *Arrested Development*, a series that aired on the Fox network that had become a cult favorite with viewers but had been canceled in 2006 after just three seasons. Netflix agreed to pay for the production of new episodes, which would begin airing in the United States in 2013.

Netflix's quest for original content continued when it debuted *Lilyhammer*, a series that features a mobster who enters the witness protection program and ends up living in Norway. Then the company ordered 13 episodes of *Orange Is the New Black*, a comedy

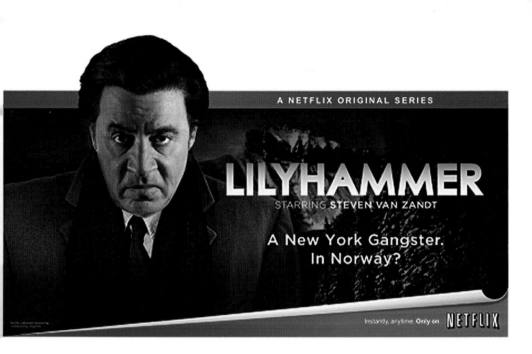

Lilyhammer, a Netflix original series, became available to Watch Instantly subscribers on February 6, 2012.

series about a suburban mom who is also a drug dealer. Next was the acquisition of 13 episodes of the thriller series *Hemlock Grove.*

Netflix was becoming very adept at choosing popular established movies and television shows to stream to their customers. The company also had the ability to estimate how popular something was likely to be among its customers. The company hoped knowledge would minimize the risk of paying for a show that turned out to be unpopular.

Netflix also minimized its advertising costs for new projects because it did not rely on traditional, large-scale marketing techniques such as television ads, billboards, and banners. Netflix simply utilized its own system of recommendations to suggest these new series to people whose viewing preferences showed they might enjoy them.

FALLING STARZ?

Netflix's quest to acquire new, original content for its online streaming came at a time when some of its previous content deals were falling through. In March 2011, Starz announced it was placing new limitations on how Netflix customers could access Starz content. Netflix users would now have a three-month delay between the release of new television shows on the Starz channel and the date they became available on Netflix.

Starz also implied a similar delay would be implemented for movies in the near future. Starz's

"I think it is healthy to have smart people make a number of negative arguments about Netflix. It sharpens our thinking."[5]

—*Reed Hastings*

restrictions on new releases were echoed by the cable channel Showtime as well. Industry experts saw these delays as cable television trying to protect itself. A writer for the *New York Times* described it this way:

> *The policy shift by Starz, a unit of Liberty Media, reflects an attitude change toward Netflix by many in Hollywood. Though Netflix, which has more than 20 million subscribers, has been embraced by media companies as a new buyer of library content, it is perceived by some of those companies as a competitive threat. Starz, after all, relies on subscriber revenue just as Netflix does.*[6]

Starz followed its announcement a few months later with the news would not be renewing its contract with Netflix when it expired in 2012. The company claimed it needed to protect its content and its cable channel. While the news resulted in a drop in value for Netflix stock, Hastings made light of the effect the loss of Starz would have on his company. He stated, "We are confident we can take the money we had earmarked for Starz renewal next year, and spend it with other content providers to maintain or even improve the Netflix experience."[7]

As confident as Hastings was, Netflix was facing a period of change. And for the first time, a company that had risen to success, despite those who said it would never last, would make some decisions that would threaten its very existence. +

In 2012, Starz did not renew its contract with Netflix.

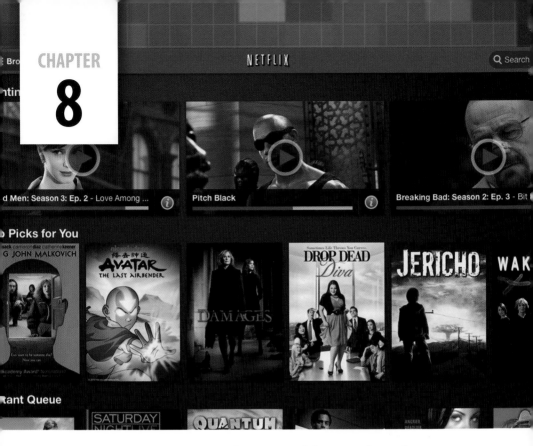

In mid-2011, Netflix announced changes to its service that would irritate thousands of subscribers.

COMPANY COLLAPSE

O n the surface, things seemed to be going well for Netflix. By early 2011, Netflix had 23.6 million subscribers. As the leading provider of DVDs and streamed movies, Netflix continued to make deals with content providers

to bring a greater variety of programming to
its customers.

Netflix, however, was finding it difficult to
provide content at the low rates its customers were
used to paying. The cost to Netflix of acquiring the
rights to produce DVDs or offer online content was
increasing all the time as the creators of movies and
television shows regularly increased their prices.

MAKING MISTAKES

On July 12, 2011, Netflix announced two significant
changes to its business. It would no longer provide
its customers with one plan, which had always
included both DVD rental and instant streaming.
Customers would have to choose either a DVD plan
or a streaming plan, with no overlap. If customers
wanted both options, they would have to maintain
two separate Netflix accounts. At the same time,
Netflix was increasing its prices. Customers who had
paid $9.99 a month for unlimited streaming and
unlimited DVD rentals would now have to pay for
two separate plans at $7.99 each, for a total cost of
$15.98 a month for both plans. In a press release on
the Netflix blog, a company spokesperson stated,

We think $7.99 is a terrific value for our unlimited streaming plan and $7.99 a terrific value for our unlimited DVD plan. We hope one, or both, of these plans makes sense for our members and their entertainment needs.[1]

"The only surprises you should give your customers are good surprises. Loyalty is a two-edged sword."[3]
—Paul Saffo, analyst, on why Netflix outraged its customers

Andy Rendich, chief service and operations officer for Netflix, added,

Netflix members love watching instantly, but we've come to recognize there is still a very large continuing demand for DVDs by mail. By better reflecting the underlying costs and offering our lowest prices ever for unlimited DVD, we hope to provide a great value to our current and future DVD-by-mail members.[2]

This showed that Netflix might have known something about the future of digital entertainment and the gradual phasing out of DVDs. However, Netflix misread its customers' willingness to make these changes. As a result, Netflix was taken by surprise at the intensity of their customers' reactions.

Netflix anticipated it would lose some of its customers with the new change in pricing and plans. It predicted a loss of approximately 5.8 percent of its customers. However, the company ended up losing 7 percent of its subscribers. Netflix was certainly not prepared for an even bigger backlash that would follow the company's second announcement in September.

THE BIG SPLIT

Two months after Netflix raised its prices on its subscription plans—when the customers were still angry about the change—Netflix announced it would be preparing for the future by completely splitting the DVD rental business from its streaming content service. The new DVD service would be called Qwikster, while the online streaming service would keep the Netflix name. It was suspected by business analysts that Netflix would eventually sell off Qwikster when it believed the DVD rental business was obsolete and no longer lucrative.

On September 19, Hastings announced the news of the Netflix split on the company blog site. He combined the announcement with an apology, which was in response to his customers'

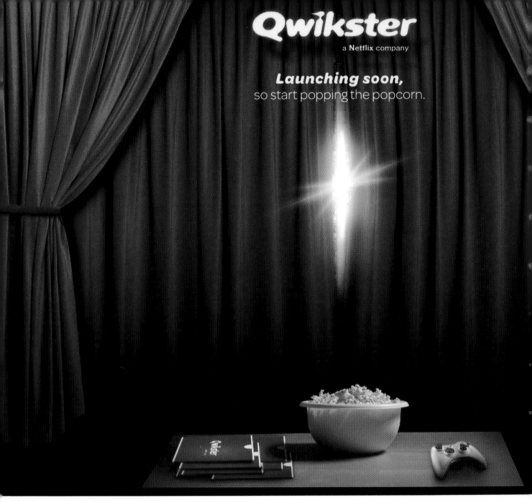

Netflix's new Web site Qwikster separated the DVD-by-mail service from the streaming video services.

outcries over recent price increases and subscription changes. "I messed up," Hastings wrote. "I owe everyone an explanation."[4] He went on to address the overwhelming backlash from subscribers over the past two months:

> *Many members felt we lacked respect and humility in the way we announced the separation of DVD*

and streaming, and the price changes. That was certainly not our intent, and I offer my sincere apology.[5]

Hastings admitted he should have personally told Netflix subscribers why DVD rentals and online streaming were being charged separately. He did confess, "It wouldn't have changed the price increase, but it would have been the right thing to do."[6]

Despite his apology, customers were furious and expressed themselves openly on the Netflix blog site as well as on social networking sites such as Facebook and Twitter. The reaction of customers to the split was even stronger than their reaction to the price increase. Many subscribers complained they would now have to use two separate Web sites and incur two separate charges on their credit cards in order to maintain the same services they had once enjoyed under one Netflix account.

TWITTER ACCOUNT

Netflix made one big mistake when it announced its plans for the new Qwikster division of its business. The company did not secure the name @Qwikster for a Twitter account, which is an essential part of Internet marketing in the twenty-first century. The Qwikster name already belonged to someone on Twitter. After the news broke, the owner demanded a large sum of money to surrender his Twitter account under that name. However, Netflix ultimately decided to use @QwiksterTweet before later deciding to abandon its plans for a Qwikster division completely.

As one analyst said, "These guys did three things bad. They raised prices. They offered lower-quality content, and they made it more complicated."[7]

NEW COKE MOMENT

Some industry analysts compared Netflix's attempt to split its brand to what Coca-Cola did in 1985. That year, Coca-Cola introduced New Coke in an attempt to replace its traditional carbonated soft drink that had been the same for nearly 100 years. The market share for original Coca-Cola had been slipping, and the company believed it was necessary to revitalize Coca-Cola. New Coke, referred to as the new taste of Coke, was a reformulated, sweeter version of the soft drink. But even though it did well in taste tests, consumers were outraged that the traditional taste of Coca-Cola was being replaced. Phone calls and letters from angry consumers flooded Coca-Cola's corporate headquarters. People ranted most about the loss of the traditional flavor. Customers purchased and hoarded cans of the old Coca-Cola. After just three months on the market, New Coke was removed, and the word *Classic* was added to all subsequent cans and bottles of the traditional soft drink. Some call the New Coke incident a huge marketing failure; others consider it a savvy marketing strategy. It increased interest in a soft drink that had been around a very long time.

One Netflix subscriber wrote on the company's blog, "On top of inconveniencing your customers, you insult us by issuing an apology way too late after the price increase. Please reconsider your move to separate the services."[8] The stock market also reflected the discontent of investors who no longer felt confident in Netflix's profitability. By October, Netflix stocks lost more than 60 percent of their value, falling from a high of $304 per share to just $77. Hastings's personal net worth fell by $640 million since he owned so many Netflix shares. Hastings commented, "We became a symbol of the evil, greedy corporation. Then we faced a reputational hit that created significantly more cancellations than we anticipated."[9] In fact, 800,000 Netflix customers, or 3 percent of its subscribers, canceled their subscriptions. Confidence in Netflix plummeted, and it was unclear if the company would ever recover.

Many experts did not think the company split had been a good idea. They pointed out that by separating the company into two individual businesses, Netflix was opening itself up to more competition from other companies. If Netflix remained unified as one large company, other companies could not so easily compete with its combined services of DVD rentals and online streaming.

ANOTHER ANNOUNCEMENT

On October 10, Netflix made another announcement. It responded to the outrage of its customers concerning the new Qwikster brand. It decided to abandon its plan to create two separate divisions, one for DVD rental and one for streaming.

BAD REPUTATION

Some analysts were not sure Netflix could ever regain its reputation after the events of 2011. Richard Pomerantz of the Strategy Group asked, "Can the company ever get back the credibility that it once had . . . if the leadership or the face of the company remains the same?"[12]

Netflix would return to its former system of allowing users to have one account and one password for both, all under the Netflix brand. Hastings remarked, "There is a difference between moving quickly—which Netflix has done very well for years—and moving too fast, which is what we did in this case."[10]

Overall, the Qwikster plan, the increase in pricing, and the extreme drop in stock prices that followed proved to Netflix it needed to pay more attention to its customers. It had to maintain a positive relationship with them, despite the company's desire to move forward with new technology and content. A professor at Boston University put it well:

> *Netflix is the latest poster child for what happens when you aggravate consumers. When you have a brand that consumers have a good relationship with—and Netflix was certainly one of those—consumers take a ton of flesh if you betray them.[11]*

Netflix subscribers let the company know they were unhappy with the $7.99 plans for streaming and DVD rental.

Netflix will need to keep customers happy to stay successful.

THE FUTURE
OF NETFLIX

Netflix certainly needed to repair its image with customers and stockholders. Both groups felt betrayed in 2011. It had been an extremely tough year for Netflix. One analyst provided some simple advice on repairing the Netflix image with consumers and stockholders: "Netflix needs to maintain the course and not do anything stupid over the next couple months."[1]

As 2012 began, Netflix struggled to maintain the wide variety of choices it provided its subscribers. Starz announced it would not renew its deal with Netflix. The agreement between the two companies expired in February 2012. Netflix also lost the right to broadcast any movies produced by Sony Pictures. There had been a clause in the Starz contract that set a cap, or limit, on the number of people who could watch Sony movies online. Netflix had exceeded that cap, and Sony movies were taken out of circulation on Netflix. Netflix downplayed the news, noting that only 8 percent of Netflix subscribers had used Starz content.

STREAMING VIDEO

By mid-2011, Netflix made deals with Sony to provide movie streaming services to Sony customers who owned PlayStation 3 and with Nintendo for the Wii. In July 2011, Netflix reported that 25 percent of its subscribers used the Wii to stream video content, making the Wii the top source for Netflix streaming.

DEALING WITH LAWSUITS

Netflix also had to deal with several lawsuits in 2011 and early 2012. Even stockholders in the company sued Netflix. They alleged the company had concealed its increasing costs to obtain content, which made the company look good to investors and inflated the price of shares. The suit also claimed that company insiders sold their own shares for the inflated prices—making approximately $90 million—before stock prices plunged following the Netflix price increase. As of early 2012, the case had not yet gone to trial.

Netflix also faced a lawsuit filed by the National Association of the Deaf (NAD), asserting the company had not provided closed captioning for all of its Watch Instantly

JOINING FACEBOOK

In June 2011, Hastings joined the board of directors of Facebook, the popular social networking site. At the time, Hastings hinted that some sort of partnership might develop between Netflix and Facebook. In a press release, Facebook's founder and CEO, Mark Zuckerberg, said, "Reed is an entrepreneur and technologist who has led Netflix to transform the way people watch movies and TV. . . . He has built a culture of continuous rapid innovation, something we share and work hard to build every day."[2] Hastings responded, "Facebook is propelling a fundamental change in how people connect with each other and share all kinds of content. . . . I'm looking forward to working with Mark and the rest of the board to help Facebook take advantage of all the opportunities ahead."[3]

In January 2012, Netflix announced it was about to implement what it called an extensive integration with Facebook. Netflix users who had Facebook accounts would be able to interact with each other, post comments and recommendations, and share their personal movie viewing history on Facebook.

movies. It claimed Netflix thus restricted certain people's access to entertainment. The NAD declared this was a violation of the Americans with Disabilities Act. A spokesperson for the NAD said,

> We have tried for years to persuade Netflix to do the right thing and provide equal access to all content across all platforms. They chose not to serve our community on an equal basis; we must have equal access to the biggest provider of streamed entertainment. . . . As Netflix itself acknowledges, streamed video is the future and we must not be left out.[4]

In November 2011, Netflix asked the court to dismiss the case, but the court denied the request. In early 2012, the case was still in progress.

Another lawsuit in 2011 involved Netflix's plan to build its

FALLING INCOME

Netflix made some changes to Hastings's income in December 2011. The changes came in part because of his role in some of the bad decisions that threatened Netflix's business. While Hastings's salary stayed at $500,000, his stock options, or the ability to buy company stock at a lower price, dropped from $3 million to $1.5 million. Basically, he was given a $1.5 million pay cut.

new corporate headquarters in Los Gatos, California. A group called Los Gatos Citizens for Responsible Development (LGCRD) sued the town of Los Gatos to slow or stop Netflix's construction because the buildings would be too tall. The group also claimed there would be too much traffic congestion, and too many trees would have to be cut down. The LGCRD maintained that it did not necessarily want to stop the construction completely, but rather it wanted the town to take time to conduct an environmental impact study. Los Gatos town manager Greg Larson remained neutral on the issue and responded that attorneys for the town are studying the matter.

LOOKING TO THE FUTURE

But despite the lawsuits, Netflix has continued to move forward. The innovative company has always been known for looking ahead to predict viewing habits and discover new technologies that might improve the Netflix experience. Hastings has realized DVDs are quickly becoming a thing of the past as more and more entertainment customers utilize online streaming. This was part of the reason Netflix changed its DVD and streaming accounts, creating so much customer concern in 2011. As one expert

A Netflix customer selects a film to stream.

in the field said, "You've got to give Reed [Hastings] credit. . . . He knows Netflix absolutely has to flee into the future with digital delivery. The problem is, not all customers have come to that yet."[5]

In January 2012, Hastings stressed DVDs are on the way out and Netflix has to cultivate instant streaming. "We expect DVD subscribers to decline steadily for every quarter, forever," Hastings said. "Our primary goal is to keep [the DVD-by-mail service] stable, very high functioning, and not to disturb it."[6] However, he also noted that Netflix would not be attempting to increase the number of DVD subscribers or market the service. However, some people say Netflix might be moving away from DVDs too quickly because the library of movies and television shows available through online streaming is not yet large enough to satisfy all customers. Netflix is also facing increasing competition from companies such as Amazon.com, Google, and Hulu, all of which also provide streaming content.

"NOW IT'S JUST PITY"

Hastings has weathered the storm with the rise and fall and recovery of Netflix with humor. When asked about the mystique that used to surround him when Netflix's fortunes were at their highest, he quipped, "Now it's just pity." But then he added, "If you fundamentally believe Internet video will change the world in 20 years, we are the leading play on that basis. As long as we don't shoot ourselves in the foot anymore."[7] Hastings has remained confident Netflix will rebound from the loss of stock value and customers, especially as it expands overseas and even into China. In the first week of 2012, Netflix stock increased almost 25 percent in value after it reported customers had streamed 2 billion hours of content in the fourth quarter of 2011.

As technology for viewing movies at home changes, Netflix is determined to keep up with the digital trends in entertainment. Netflix still hopes to split its household accounts into individual user accounts. After all, as household members increasingly use mobile devices such as smartphones and tablet computers, they are more likely to watch movies separately.

But Netflix has certainly learned it will also have to keep its customers very happy. With all the changes, the company is committed to maintaining the services customers prefer. It will try to please its customers who still prefer DVDs as well as the ones who want more online streaming and the latest technologies.

"I think there will be 20 years of evolution from linear broadcast to Internet television. In 20 years from now we will all be able to click and watch TV. Broadcast TV is like the landline of 20 years ago. I think of [Netflix] as like mobile—today all of the interesting things are happening in mobile."[8]

—*Reed Hastings on the evolution of television*

"Once you subscribe, our interest is purely your happiness."[10]

—*Reed Hastings*

Hastings said, "Our task is to consistently improve the quality of our service and stay two steps ahead."[9] Going forward, Netflix plans to avoid any more tumbles and falls by staying focused on its customers and on the ideas and philosophies that have made it such an incredibly successful company. +

With smartphones, Netflix online streaming customers
can watch movies anywhere.

TIMELINE

1958	1960	1979

Marc Randolph is born on April 29.

Wilmot Reed Hastings Jr. is born in Belmont, Massachusetts, on October 8.

Hastings attends Bowdoin College in Brunswick, Maine.

1991	1996	1997

Hastings starts Pure Software in October.

Randolph joins the staff at Pure Atria Software.

The digital versatile disc (DVD) player debuts.

1981

Randolph graduates from Hamilton College in Clinton, New York.

1983

Hastings joins the Peace Corps and teaches math in Africa.

1988

Hastings graduates from Stanford University in California with a master's degree in computer science.

1997

Hastings sells Pure Atria and starts Netflix with Randolph.

1998

The Netflix Web site goes live on April 14.

1999

Netflix launches its subscription service on September 23.

TIMELINE

2002	2003	2004

Netflix goes public on the stock exchange.

Netflix reaches 1 million subscribers.

Randolph retires from Netflix.

2008	2010	2011

Netflix joins with Microsoft to provide movie services to Xbox 360 users.

Fortune magazine names Reed Hastings 2010 Businessperson of the Year.

Netflix announces a price hike on July 12.

2006

Netflix launches a $1 million contest to find a new algorithm for recommending movies.

2008

Netflix offers Watch Instantly, an online streaming service.

2008

Netflix eliminates the Profiles feature and faces negative customer feedback. Netflix quickly restores Profiles.

2011

In September, Netflix apologizes for the price hike and announces a split in the DVD and streaming services.

2011

On October 10, Netflix changes its mind about splitting into two services.

2012

Netflix announces a partnership with Facebook for the near future.

ESSENTIAL FACTS

CREATORS

Wilmot Reed Hastings Jr. (October 8, 1960–)

Marc Randolph (April 29, 1958–)

DATE LAUNCHED

April 4, 1998

CHALLENGES

Netflix started its DVD-by-mail service at a time when DVD players were a new technology and not widely available. Although it became the leading DVD rental-by-mail company, Netflix has struggled to balance this technology with the growing popularity of instant online streaming, trying to keep both types of customers happy. It has also faced continued challenges from competitors such as Amazon.com, Google, and Hulu, as well as the increasing costs of providing more movie and television content for its users. Netflix has had to change its terms and policies as a result of several lawsuits. But the company faced its biggest challenge when its customers turned against Netflix after the company announced it would raise prices and split its services into two divisions, DVD and online streaming. More than 800,000 subscribers left Netflix.

SUCCESSES

Since Netflix went live in April 1998, the company has attracted 23.6 million subscribers who have enjoyed the company's flat-fee model for unlimited movie rentals with no late fees or shipping fees. Netflix's success also comes from its features, including a personalized movie recommendation service based on other subscribers' reviews. The company has boosted its appeal by entering into agreements with the movie and television industries to provide customers with premium movies and television series. Netflix is among the most successful dot-com businesses. It continues to be a leader in providing DVD rentals by mail as well as instant online streaming. It has also become a distributor for lesser-known and independent films as well as new content.

IMPACT ON SOCIETY

Netflix's business model of subscription-based movie rentals for a flat fee has been widely copied by other ventures. The company has changed the way people access and watch movies and television, and it has made entertainment instantly available and affordable.

QUOTE

"Our task is to consistently improve the quality of our service and stay two steps ahead."

—*Reed Hastings*

GLOSSARY

algorithm
> A set of rules that specifies how a computer should do something or solve a problem.

backlash
> A strong or violent reaction, especially in response to a social or political change.

debug
> To identify and remove errors from computers.

digital
> Involving or relating to the use of computer technology.

lucrative
> Profitable or moneymaking.

media
> Means of communication such as radio, television, and newspapers that reach a large number of people.

network
> A group of television or broadcasting stations that distributes television content at the same time.

paramount
> Most important, supreme, or superior.

queue
> A line or list; a sequence of items on a Web site.

smartphone

A mobile phone with computerlike features including e-mail, Internet, and a personal organizer.

software

The programs used to direct the operations of a computer.

stock

A share of a particular company that represents a small amount of ownership of that company.

streaming

Transmission of data in real time, especially over the Internet.

subscription

An arrangement in which a consumer pays a set amount per month in exchange for services or items such as magazines or newspapers.

synchronized

Occurring at the same time; operating simultaneously or in unison.

tablet

A small rectangular computer that is extremely thin and light.

ADDITIONAL RESOURCES

SELECTED BIBLIOGRAPHY

Conlin, Michelle. "Netflix: Flex to the Max." *Bloomberg Businessweek*, 24 Sept. 2007. Web. 25 Jan. 2012.

Copeland, Michael V. "Reed Hastings: Leader of the Pack." *CNN Money*, 18 Nov. 2010. Web. 27 Jan. 2012.

Kuang, Cliff. "5 Ways Netflix Could Have Avoided an Ugly User Backlash." *Fast Company*, 16 March 2010. Web. 27 Jan. 2012.

O'Brien, Jeffrey M. "The Netflix Effect." *Wired*, Dec. 2002. Web. 25 Jan. 2012.

FURTHER READINGS

Benjamin, Daniel. *Pop Culture in America: American Life and Movies from the Ten Commandments to Twilight*. Pelham, NY: Benchmark Education, 2012. Print.

Brasch, Nicolas. *The Technology behind the Internet*. Mankato, MN: Smart Apple Media, 2011. Print.

Conley, Robyn. *Motion Pictures*. New York: Scholastic, 2004. Print.

Rowell, Rebecca. *YouTube: The Company and Its Founders*. Minneapolis, MN: Abdo, 2011. Print.

WEB LINKS

To learn more about Netflix, visit ABDO Publishing Company online at **www.abdopublishing.com**. Web sites about Netflix are featured on our Book Links page. These links are routinely monitored and updated to provide the most current information available.

PLACES TO VISIT

Computer History Museum
1401 N. Shoreline Boulevard
Mountain View, CA 94043
650-810-1010
http://www.computerhistory.org
The Computer History Museum is the world's premier museum documenting and exploring the history of computing and its impact on society.

The Hollywood Museum
1660 N. Highland Avenue
Hollywood, CA 90028
323-464-7776
http://thehollywoodmuseum.com
The Hollywood Museum features hundreds of exhibits that showcase the history of movies, costuming, makeup, and props. The historic collection presents an up-close look at the world of film.

Netflix Headquarters
100 Winchester Circle
Los Gatos, CA 95032
408-540-3700
http://www.Netflix.com
The Netflix corporate headquarters employs approximately 900 people and serves as a distribution center for mailing out DVDs to subscribers.

SOURCE NOTES

CHAPTER 1. INSTANT MOVIES

1. Michael V. Copeland. "Reed Hastings: Leader of the Pack." *Fortune*. Cable News Network, 18 Nov. 2010. Web. 21 Feb. 2012.

2. Ibid.

3. Ibid.

4. Patrick J. Sauer. "How I Did It: Reed Hastings, Netflix." *Inc.* Mansueto Ventures, 1 Dec. 2005. Web. 14 Mar. 2012.

5. Trefis. "Netflix: Missteps Behind, Opportunity Ahead." *MSN Money*. Microsoft, 4 Jan. 2012. Web. 29 Feb. 2012.

CHAPTER 2. ENTERTAINMENT EVOLUTION

None

CHAPTER 3. THE MEN BEHIND NETFLIX

1. Matthew Boyle. "Questions for . . . Reed Hastings." *CNN Money*. Cable News Network, 23 May 2007. Web. 14 Mar. 2012.

2. Michelle Conlin. "Netflix: Flex to the Max." *Bloomberg Businessweek*. Bloomberg, 24 Sept. 2007. Web. 14 Mar. 2012.

3. Marc Randolph. "Want to Learn to Be a Leader? Just Be One." *Kibble [Marc Randolph Personal Blog]*. Kibble, 13 Feb. 2012. Web. 18 Apr. 2012.

4. Ibid.

5. Daniel Schorn. "The Brain behind Netflix." *60 Minutes*. CBS Interactive, 11 Feb. 2009. Web. 14 Mar. 2012.

6. Ibid.

7. Stacey Grenrock Woods. "Science and Industry: Reed Hastings." *Esquire*. Hearst Communications, 1 Dec. 2005. Web. 18 Apr. 2012.

CHAPTER 4. GOING LIVE

1. "How Netflix Got Started." *CNN Money*. Cable News Network, 28 Jan. 2009. Web. 13 Mar. 2012.

2. "DVD Terms and Conditions." *Netflix*. Netflix, n.d. Web. 2 Feb. 2012.

3. Jeffrey M. O'Brien. "The Netflix Effect." *Wired*. Condé Nast, Dec. 2002. Web. 9 Mar. 2012.

4. "How Netflix Got Started." *CNN Money*. Cable News Network, 28 Jan. 2009. Web. 13 Mar. 2012.

5. Ibid.

6. Ibid.

7. Michael V. Copeland. "Reed Hastings: Leader of the Pack." *Fortune*. Cable News Network, 18 Nov. 2010. Web. 21 Feb. 2012.

8. Henry Blodget. "How Netflix Conquered the World: Management Secrets that Propelled a DVD-by-Mail Company to Greatness." *Business Insider*. Business Insider, 4 Apr. 2011. Web. 13 Mar. 2012.

9. Michael Gillis. "Head in the Cloud." *Cornell University, College of Engineering News and Events*. Cornell University, Fall 2011. Web. 25 Feb. 2012.

CHAPTER 5. CONNECTING WITH STARZ

1. Darren Murph. "Starz Play Content Added to Netflix's Streaming Library." *engadget*. AOL, 1 Oct. 2008. Web. 25 Feb. 2012.

2. "Netflix Unveils Profiles." *PR Newswire*. PR Newswire, 18 Jan. 2005. Web. 11 Mar. 2012.

3. Michael Gillis. "Head in the Cloud." *Cornell University, College of Engineering News and Events*. Cornell University, Fall 2011. Web. 25 Feb. 2012.

4. "Profiles Feature NOT Going Away." *Netflix*. Netflix, 30 June 2008. Web. 8 Feb. 2012.

5. Ibid.

CHAPTER 6. DEALS AND MORE DEALS

1. Cliff Kuang. "5 Ways Netflix Could Have Avoided an Ugly User Backlash." *Fast Company*. Mansueto Ventures, 16 Mar. 2010. Web. 8 Feb. 2012.

2. Ibid.

SOURCE NOTES CONTINUED

CHAPTER 7. ORIGINAL CONTENT

1. Michael V. Copeland. "Reed Hastings: Leader of the Pack." *Fortune*. Cable News Network, 18 Nov. 2010. Web. 21 Feb. 2012.

2. Ibid.

3. MG Siegler. "Netflix Original Content Is Much More Than a Strategy Shift—It Could Shift an Industry." *TechCrunch*. AOL, 18 Mar. 2011. Web. 28 Feb. 2012.

4. Ibid.

5. Michael V. Copeland. "Reed Hastings: Leader of the Pack." *Fortune*. Cable News Network, 18 Nov. 2010. Web. 21 Feb. 2012.

6. Brian Stelter. "Starz to Delay Release of Shows on Netflix." *New York Times*. New York Times, 24 Mar. 2011. Web. 13 Mar. 2012.

7. Andrew Wallenstein. "Starz Nixes Deal with Netflix." *Variety*. Reed Elsevier, 1 Sept. 2011. Web. 12 Jan. 2012.

CHAPTER 8. COMPANY COLLAPSE

1 "Netflix Introduces New Plans and Announces Price Changes." *Netflix*. Netflix, 12 July 2011. Web. 25 Jan. 2012.

2. Catharine Smith. "Netflix Announces Price Hike, New Subscription Plans." *Huffington Post*. Huffington Post, 12 July 2011. Web. 1 Mar. 2012.

3. Ronald Grover and Cliff Edwards. "Can Netflix Find Its Future by Abandoning the Past?" *Bloomberg Businessweek*. Bloomberg, 22 Sept. 2011. Web. 11 Mar. 2012.

4. Reed Hastings. "An Explanation and Some Reflections." *Netflix*. Netflix, 18 Sept. 2011. Web. 4 Mar. 2012.

5. Ibid.

6. Ibid.

7. Scott Martin and Mike Snider. "Netflix Splits DVD, Streaming Businesses." *USA Today*. Gannett, 19 Sept. 2011. Web. 9 Mar. 2012.

8. Ibid.

9. Stacy Curtin. "A 'Spectacular' Collapse." *Yahoo! Finance*. Yahoo, 25 Oct. 2011. Web. 12 Feb. 2012.

10. Logan Burruss and David Goldman. "Netflix Abandons Plan for Qwikster DVD Service." *CNN Money*. Cable News Network, 10 Oct. 2011. Web. 13 Mar. 2012.

11. Ibid.

12. Mike Snider. "Netflix Axes Qwikster; Kills Plan to Split in Two." *USA Today*. Gannett, 10 Oct. 2011. Web. 11 Mar. 2012.

CHAPTER 9. THE FUTURE OF NETFLIX

1. Mike Snider. "Netflix Axes Qwikster; Kills Plan to Split in Two." *USA Today*. Gannett, 10 Oct. 2011. Web. 11 Mar. 2012.

2. "Facebook Names Reed Hastings to Its Board of Directors." *PR Newswire*. PR Newswire, 23 June 2011. Web. 11 Mar. 2012.

3. Ibid.

4. Lance Whitney. "Netflix Sued by Deaf Group over Lack of Subtitles." *CNET*. CBS Interactive, 20 June 2011. Web. 12 Mar. 2012.

5. Ronald Grover and Cliff Edwards. "Can Netflix Find Its Future by Abandoning the Past?" *Bloomberg Businessweek*. Bloomberg, 22 Sept. 2011. Web. 3 Feb. 2012.

6. Brent Lang. "Netflix CEO Reed Hastings: 'We Expect DVD Subscribers to Decline Forever.'" *Reuters*. Thomson Reuters, 25 Jan. 2012. Web. 13 Mar. 2012.

7. Michael Liedtke. "Netflix CEO Reed Hastings on Mistakes, Biggest Competition." *Huff Post Tech*. Huffington Post, 7 Dec. 2011. Web. 22 Feb. 2012.

8. Dan Sabbagh. "Reed Hastings Interview: 'Everybody Would Welcome a Rival to Sky.'" *The Guardian*. Guardian News and Media, 15 Jan. 2012. Web. 13 Mar. 2012.

9. Ronald Grover and Cliff Edwards. "Can Netflix Find Its Future by Abandoning the Past?" *Bloomberg Businessweek*. Bloomberg, 22 Sept. 2011. Web. 3 Feb. 2012.

10. Ricky W. Griffin. *Organizational Behavior: Managing People and Organizations*. Mason, OH: South-Western College, 2012. Print. 231.

INDEX

algorithm contest, 43–44

Ampex Corporation, 17

BellKor's Pragmatic Chaos, 44

Betamax, 18

bundling, 70

cable television, 20–21, 49–50, 57, 73

CineMatch, 42–43, 44

Cloud storage, 50

CV-2000, 17–18

digital versatile disc (DVD) player, 19–20, 32

digital versatile discs (DVDs), 19, 31–32, 35, 36, 41, 47, 51, 77, 79, 83, 90, 93

entertainment, changes in, 14–15

Friends feature, 58–60

Hastings, Reed
   Apollo 13 rental, 30–31
   apologies, 79–81, 83–84
   education, 25, 26, 29–30
   Facebook board of directors, 88

family, 24–25

financial losses, 11, 89

Fortune's Businessperson of the Year, 6, 7, 11, 66

Netflix CEO, 6, 34

Netflix chairman of the board, 34

Peace Corps, 25–26

Hulu, 60, 92

Jaws, 20

LaserDisc, 20

movie industry, 15–16, 57

movie rental stores, 18, 32, 39, 44, 62–63

Netflix
   competition, 60–63, 92
   customer dissatisfaction, 11, 52–54, 58–60, 78–79, 81–84, 86–87
   deals with other companies, 56–58, 68–69, 76–77, 87
   distribution facilities, 35, 40
   envelopes, 8, 36–37, 39, 46–47
   idea, 30, 31–32
   lawsuits, 36, 87–90

name, 35

pricing, 77–79, 80

stock prices, 41, 61, 67, 82, 92–93

Web site, 8, 30, 32, 34, 40, 42, 58, 59, 61

work atmosphere, 40–41

original content, 68–71

pay-per-view, 20–21

Profiles, 51–54

Pure Software, 26–27, 29

Qwikster, 79, 81, 83–84

Randolph, Marc

education, 28–29

leadership camp, 28

marketing career, 29

Netflix CEO, 34

Netflix cofounder, 8, 27, 32, 34

Netflix executive producer, 35

rentals by mail, 10, 35, 36, 39, 47, 48, 51, 58, 78, 79, 81, 92

smartphone, 9, 22, 93

Sony, 17–18, 87

Starz contract, 49–51, 72–73, 87

streaming, 7, 9, 10, 21–22, 47–48, 49–51, 56, 57–58, 60, 63, 64, 72, 77, 79, 81, 83, 87, 90–92, 93

subscription service, 37–38, 39

television, 11, 15, 16–17

throttling, 36

Twitter account, 81

Video Home System (VHS), 18

videocassette recorder (VCR), 18–20

videocassettes, 18, 20, 31–32, 39

videotape recorder (VTR), 16–18

Watch Instantly, 47–48, 51, 68, 88–89

ABOUT THE AUTHOR

Marcia Amidon Lusted is the author of more than 65 books for young readers, as well as hundreds of magazine articles. She is an assistant editor for Cobblestone Publishing, a writing instructor, and a musician. She lives in New Hampshire with her family.

PHOTO CREDITS

The Canadian Press, Adrien Veczan/AP Images, cover; Martin E. Klimek/ZUMA Press/Alamy, 6; Matthew J. Lee/The Boston Globe/Getty Images, 9; Paul Sakuma/AP Images, 13, 46, 66, 91, 98 (bottom); AP Images, 14, 17; Susan Daniels/iStockphoto, 19, 96 (bottom); Michael Willis/Alamy, 23; Robert F. Bukaty/AP Images, 24, 96 (top); Douglas C. Pizac/AP Images, 30; Netflix, Jack Dempsey/AP Images, 33; Justin Sullivan/Getty Images, 34, 38, 98 (top); Jason Kempin/Getty Images, 45; PRNewsFoto/Lionsgate/AP Images, 49; Netflix Inc./AP Images, 55, 80, 97 (bottom), 99; Andrew Harrer/Bloomberg/Getty Images, 56; Frances Roberts/Alamy, 62; Marcio Jose Sanchez/AP Images, 65; PRNewsFoto/Netflix, Inc./AP Images, 71, 76; PRNewsFoto/Starz Entertainment/AP Images, 75; digitallife/Alamy, 85; Shutterstock Images, 86; Tryphosa Ho/Alamy, 95